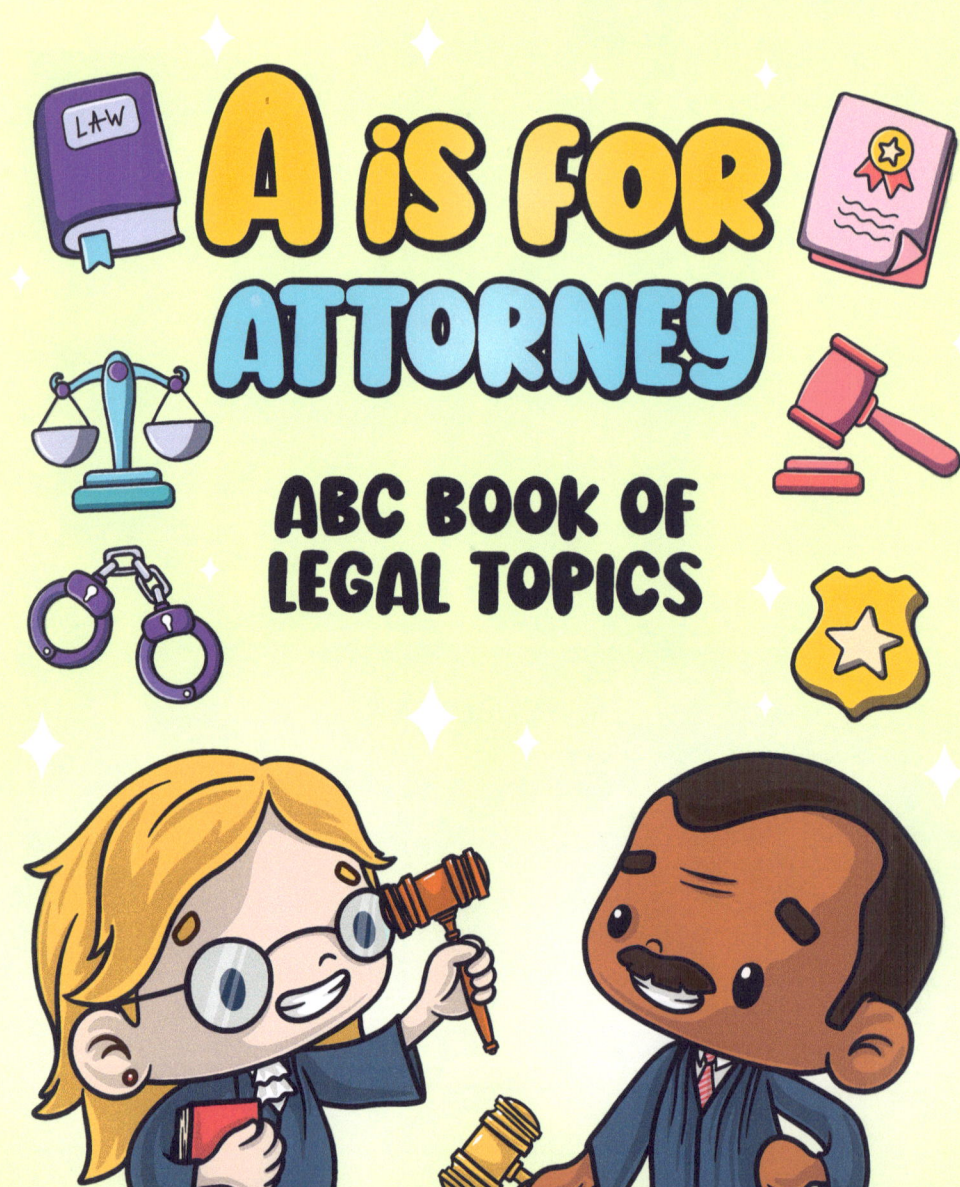

THIS BOOK BELONGS TO:

ISBN: 9798880077908

A

is for attorney

a legal hero who helps people solve problems and protect their rights in court.

B

is for bailiff

a courtroom guardian who makes sure everyone behaves and follows the rules.

C

is for contract

a special promise that two people make to each other, like promising to share toys fairly.

D

is for defendant

someone who gets into trouble and has to explain what happened to a judge.

E

is for evidence

important clues like fingerprints or footprints that help solve mysteries.

F

is for felony

a really big no-no that means breaking a very serious rule.

G

is for guardian

a grown-up who keeps you safe and helps you grow up strong.

H

is for habeas corpus

a special paper that helps someone prove they shouldn't be kept in a dungeon, like a key to unlock the door to freedom.

I

is for indictment

a fancy word for accusing someone of doing something wrong.

J

is for judge

a wise and fair ruler of the courtroom who helps solve problems and keeps everyone safe.

K

is for knowledge

learning new things every day, like
discovering the ABCs of the legal way.

L

is for litigation

a big adventure where people go to court to
solve their problems with the help of a judge.

M

is for mediation

a peaceful way to settle disagreements without fighting, like using words instead of swords.

N

is for notary

a person who makes sure important papers are real and true, like a magical seal of approval.

O

is for objection

a strong "no way!" that someone says in court when they think something isn't fair.

P

is for plaintiff

a brave person who goes to court to ask for
help when something isn't right.

Q

is for questioning

a curious time in court when people ask and answer lots of important questions.

R

is for restitution

a special way to say "I'm sorry" by making
things right when something goes wrong.

S

is for subpoena

a magical summons that calls someone to court like a royal invitation.

T

is for trial

a big show in court where everyone tells their side of the story and a wise judge decides what's fair.

U

is for unlawful

a fancy way to say breaking the rules and doing things that are not allowed.

V

is for verdict

the big decision made by a judge or jury
after hearing all the facts.

W

is for warrant

a magical paper that lets authorities take action, like a key to open the doors of justice.

X

is for exhibit

a special show-and-tell in court where important clues are shared to solve the mystery.

Y

is for youth court

a special place where young people learn
about rules and consequences in a safe way.

Z

is for zeal

having a lot of passion and enthusiasm, like a superhero fighting for justice with all their might.